Education

Green Box Kids
Learn About Compromise

A comic book-based social skills curriculum

Written by:
Carl Dzyak, M.Ed., BCBA, LBA
Barbara Kaminski, Ph.D., BCBA-D, LBA
Christopher Richardson, M.Ed., BCBA, LBA

Illustrated by:
Sarah Miller

www.greenboxABA.org

www.facebook.com/GreenBoxABA

www.twitter.com/GreenBoxEdu

This book is dedicated to the cool kids who do the awesome things that inspire us every day.

Green Box
Education

Table of Contents

Introduction

Welcome To The Green Box Social Skills Curriculum!

Each volume of the curriculum concentrates on a specific social skill that may present a challenge, particularly for a child with special needs. Each of the three lessons in every volume consists of a comic and activities. The comics feature the Green Box Kids in challenging social scenarios. The interactions are presented with minimal text in a child-friendly, visually-striking format to help engage the student in the social lesson with ease and enjoyment.

Social Skills Are Foundational!

Family. School. Neighborhoods. Sports Teams. Clubs. The enjoyment and success of participating in such social groups is related, in many ways, to the ability to function in social settings. Given the amount of time spent in social groups, both as a child and into adulthood, learning social skills is a vital component of a child's overall development.

Social Skills Impairments in Children with Special Needs

While all children sometimes experience difficulties navigating complicated social situations, the child with special needs often needs extra help and support. Research has shown social skills impairments in children diagnosed with conduct disorders, mood disorders, anxiety disorders, autism spectrum disorders, attention-deficit/hyperactivity disorder (ADHD), learning disabilities, and other behavioral challenges (Rutherford et al., 2004).

Typical deficits include difficulty initiating and responding in social interactions, making and maintaining eye contact, reading non-verbal cues (including facial expressions and body language), taking another person's perspective, recognizing feelings, and knowing what to talk about and for how long.

Consequences of Social Skills Impairments

When supported learning opportunities are not provided, the lack of positive peer interactions can lead to avoidance of social opportunities and a downward spiral, as fewer opportunities for learning are encountered. This makes it difficult for a child to develop and maintain meaningful personal relationships. Often, as a result, these children gravitate towards solitary play and activities.

Teaching Social Skills

Finding ways and opportunities to practice social interaction skills in a supportive environment can be difficult. However, while not as straightforward to teach as, for example, multiplication facts, social skills can be taught and strengthened. Children with special learning needs may require intentional instruction that can include modeling, role playing social scenarios, social stories, and instruction based on the techniques and principles of Applied Behavior Analysis.

What Is Applied Behavior Analysis?

Conceptual Foundation

Based on learning theory (Skinner, 1953), Applied Behavior Analysis (ABA) is a scientific approach for teaching new skills and decreasing behaviors that are harmful or interfere with learning.

Because of its scientific foundation, ABA focuses on measurable behavior change that is the result of events that occur before and/or after a behavior (Baer et al, 1968). Events that occur after a behavior and increase its likelihood of reoccurring are called reinforcers. On the other hand, punishment after a behavior decreases the likelihood it will occur again.

Teaching Strategies

ABA Practitioners (Board Certified Behavior Analysts or BCBAs) use many different teaching strategies. These include specific instructional techniques, such as direct instruction and discrete trial training. "Shaping," the process of teaching closer and closer approximations to the desired skill, is a commonly used technique. Another is "chaining," in which smaller skills are learned and linked together to accomplish a larger task.

However, ABA is not a "one size fits all" approach; because the needs for each child are different, the goals and strategies used to achieve them are individually tailored for each child. Progress is continuously measured and modifications to goals and strategies are based on the measured outcomes, resulting in efficient and effective treatment.

Goals

ABA has been used to help improve the lives of individuals by focusing on behaviors that are socially significant for the individual. A wide variety of different skills, such as communication & language skills, academics, self-help skills, work skills, domestic and life skills, self-monitoring, play skills, and social skills have been taught using ABA strategies. ABA principles have also been used to help decrease problematic behaviors, such as self-injury and aggression. In all cases, the goal is to bring about meaningful and positive behavior change.

Overview of the Green Box Kids Social Skills Curriculum

Developed by a team of BCBAs and professional artists, the Green Box Kids Social Skills Curriculum and supplemental materials support a comprehensive approach to social skills training. Although the curriculum evolved from application of principles of behavior analysis, no special training in ABA is necessary to use the materials. Our mission is to provide professionals, including speech and language pathologists, special educators, psychologists, counselors, and applied behavior analysts with engaging tools that are inherently motivating for learners. Additionally, we aim to provide parents with the tools they need to address social skills challenges, even if they cannot access private therapy on their own.

Relatable Characters

The Green Box Kids Social Skills Curriculum offers a unique approach to social skills lessons by introducing relatable characters that are easy for children to connect with. The Green Box Kids are a group of elementary school-aged friends who deal with the kinds of social skills challenges that many students regularly encounter. Each of the kids has

unique likes, dislikes, strengths, and challenges that define them. As learners get to know each character, they may find themselves relating to their favorite Green Box Kids' quirks and idiosyncrasies. Just like regular kids, the Green Box Kids are not perfect.

Realistic Scenarios in Comic Book Format

The art in the Green Box Kids curriculum is presented in a comic book format. Unlike other popular materials, the lessons contain minimal text, which allows learners to easily navigate social lessons without being burdened with unnecessary language. Because the kids look and act like real kids participating in real life scenarios, students have the opportunity to observe and reflect on realistic facial expressions and body language, which are critical building blocks to social development.

Active Responding and Practice

Through active responding and practice, the activities in the book create opportunities for new skills to be acquired and strengthened in a supported environment that promotes successful social interactions. Real world social interactions are often complex, unpredictable, and varied. To reflect this, an answer key is not included for these activities, leaving flexibility for answers based on the varied, but appropriate, ways to react to a social situation.

Meet the Kids! Cami, Mei, Lucy, Tito, Barry, Richard, Jack, and Lisa

Green Box Education

Compromise

In each of the three social comics and lessons in this volume, the Green Box Kids learn more about what it means to **compromise** and why it is important. The ability to compromise is a vital life and social skill that children need to learn in order to make and keep friends and in a social setting, such as a classroom. While compromise can be a challenge, it can be learned and developed with practice and support.

A compromise is an agreement during a dispute that is reached by both sides making concessions. Sometimes that means finding a "middle ground." Other times it means one person gets what they want now in exchange for the other person getting what they want later. The lessons in this volume help children learn how to ask to compromise and how to respond when others ask. They will learn, for example, that compromise does not involve one person "giving in" and that everyone needs to be involved in the decision. Because the comics show the reactions of all of the people involved in the social interaction, each lesson helps the learner recognize the social consequences of compromising with others and of not compromising. The supporting activities walk your learner though the concept of compromise as they compare what they are learning to what happens to their favorite Green Box Kids characters.

How To Use This Book

The Green Box Kids Social Skills Curriculum is ideally used in a group setting with similar-aged peers and/or other children at a comparable developmental level. Group settings provide opportunities for discussion, sharing of ideas and real-life scenarios, and active practice of the skills. However, the materials can be used individually, for example, in the home, with the parent filling the role of the social "peer."

Each lesson focuses on a different component of the social skill. However, all of the lessons are set-up in the same format. Each lesson consists of:

Warm-Up Questions

Each lesson starts with a series of "warm-up" questions about the topic. Use these questions to find out how much the learner already knows about the topic that will be covered. These questions introduce the topic and will be answered in the course of the lesson, so you don't need to spend too much time discussing them.

The Comic

In 6 – 7 panels, the comic sets up a socially-based problem and an "inappropriate" solution to the problem.

Breakdown of Comic, Panel By Panel

The comic is broken down, panel by panel, with 1 – 2 questions that encourage the learner to concentrate on social cues (facial expressions, body language) for clues. This facilitates conversation about and engagement with the characters' feelings and reactions.

Follow-up Questions

A series of follow-up questions are included to check comprehension of the events and concepts presented in the comic.

Learning Activities

Two to three learning activities, presented in a variety of learning formats, provide practice with the social concepts. Many of the activities are designed to be completed with a partner or group, opening the door for application and practice of the skill.

Solution Comic & Wrap-up Discussion

Each lesson ends with an opportunity for the learner to draw a comic panel with a guess about an a solution to the social problem. An appropriate solution comic is then presented, along with 1 or 2 questions designed to wrap-up the lesson. You may also go back and ask the Warm-up Questions again to see how much the student has learned.

Tips

- Use social praise for appropriate responses and interactions.
- Although space has been provided for written answers, learners may either write in their own answers or give them verbally, depending on skill level.
- If used in a group, as the adult you should be sure to function as a discussion leader
   o Encourage the group to go beyond just answering the question and to "dig deeper"
   o During the discussion, relate the answers to real-life examples
   o Don't let the discussion get off-topic
   o Don't let one or two kids dominate the discussion
   o Find ways to involve everyone in the group discussion and activities
- Provide guidance and prompts/suggestions, as needed. But encourage peer facilitation.
- Whenever possible, find ways during the lessons to provide opportunities to practice the skill in the social group setting.

How To Measure Progress

Measuring progress is an essential component of any curriculum. Below is guidance for measuring progress. For parents or educators with little to no experience in Applied Behavior Analysis (ABA), we have included a straightforward and easy way to measure development of skills (Appendix A). Progress in the school setting can be measured by including a compromise goal on the child's Individualized Education Program (IEP). Some suggested IEP goals can be found in Appendix B. For ABA professionals and educators with more experience in ABA, a more detailed behavior change program is outlined in Appendix C.

Let's say that you want to know if a child is making progress in learning math facts. A common assessment method is the "speed drill," in which the child is given 1 minute to complete a worksheet with 100 math problems. It is not unusual to administer a speed drill before any instruction begins (a "pretest", in order to determine how much the child already knows. The speed drill may be given weekly, until the child receives a particular score (for example, at least 90 correct out of 100).

Measuring progress made while learning social skills is a bit more complex but conceptually the same. There are two things that you will need to decide: (1) what to measure and (2) when to measure.

What to Measure

Progress should be shown not only in how a learner answers the questions in this book but also in development of overall skills. We recommend using the materials found in Appendix A to assess overall skill development. The rating scale and checklist help determine how much the child has learned about how to ask appropriately to compromise, what to do when someone does not want to compromise or offers solutions they don't like, what to do when you don't want to compromise, and how to remain calm while in compromise situations..

When to Measure

As with the speed drills, it is best to first determine what the child already knows or can do. Therefore, we recommend assessing the current skill level before you begin using the materials. Then, after the book has been completed, assess how much the child has learned. Because each of the lessons in this book focus on a different component of the social skill, you could do a learning check after each lesson, similar to administering speed drills once a week.

Summary and Extension

After this book has been completed, the learner should have a greater understanding of the targeted social skill and the ways in which it is important for developing and maintaining relationships with others. Additionally, the child will have learned some strategies related to displaying the skill. However, social skill development is a process and you should continue to provide opportunities for practice. Children who are still developing foundational social skills often feel more comfortable in small groups. Regardless of the group size, try to make the environment comfortable and supportive, while providing feedback, guidance, and praise for appropriate behaviors. Finally, don't forget that adult behavior can provide a good example of how to respond to social situations, so find and use opportunities to model appropriate responses.

References

Baer, D.M., Wolf, M.M., & Risley, T.R., (1968). Some current dimensions of applied behavior analysis. *Journal of Applied Behavior Analysis*, 1, 91-97.

Rutherford, R.B.Jr., Quinn, M.M., & Mathur, S.R. (2004). Handbook of Research in Emotional and Behavioral Disorders. New York, NY: The Guilford Press.

Skinner, B.F. (1953). Science and Human Behavior. New York, NY: The MacMillian Press.

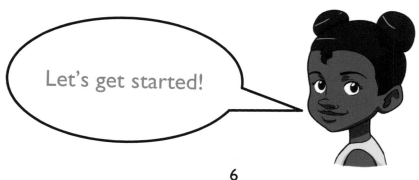

Let's get started!

Let's Learn About Compromise
Lesson 1: The Pizza

Find out what you already know about compromise.

1. What does it mean to compromise?

_____

_____

_____

2. What kinds of things do friends disagree about?

_____

_____

_____

3. How can you tell someone you want to compromise?

_____

_____

_____

4. What is something that you should not compromise about?

_____

_____

_____

5. You and your friend are riding bikes up a steep hill. Your friend wants to ride up to the top and then ride down fast. You are very tired and don't want to go any higher. You and your friend have to stay together. What could you do?

_____

_____

_____

Lesson 1: The Pizza

Read the comic on the following page about Tito, Richard, and Lisa to learn about a time when compromise did not go so well. Make sure to look closely at the Green Box Kids' faces to see how they may be feeling.

Let's Break It Down!

Now we are going to break the comic down to get a better idea of what

is going on in each picture.

What's happening in this picture?

What is Tito doing?

How does Lisa feel?

What part of Richard's face lets you know he does not like spices?

Does Tito feel the same or different from his friends? How do you know?

What is happening in this picture?

Let's Think About It.

The questions on the following page will help us better understand the

comic we just read.

Answer the following questions about the comic you just read. Some questions may have more than one right answer.

1. What ingredients did Richard and Lisa not want to have on the pizza?

_____

_____

_____

2. Why did Tito decide to make pizza with peppers and onions?

_____

_____

_____

3. Do you think Richard and Lisa are being selfish by asking Tito to leave those ingredients off the pizza? Why do you think that?

_____

_____

_____

4. Do you think Tito is being selfish? Why do you think that?

_____

_____

_____

5. How did Richard and Lisa feel about the pizza that Tito made?

_____

_____

_____

6. What do you think Tito could say to make his friends feel better?

_____

_____

_____

7. Should all three of them stay friends after this situation?

_____

_____

_____

8. Is there a way they could still include onions and peppers on the pizza and still include Richard and Lisa?

_____

_____

_____

9. If they decide to make another pizza together, what should they do first?

_____

_____

_____

10. If you decide to make a pizza with your friends, what will you do first?

_____

_____

_____

Compromise is wise!

Compromising helps us to keep our friends and family happy. It also helps keep you happy. In the next section we will talk about how compromise affects relationships.

Talk about it with your friends!

How do you feel when you are left out of a decision?

How do you feel when others include you in their decision and try to make you happy?

We're going on a camping trip! We need to pack our bags. Find a partner and, using compromise, choose 5 items that you think would be the most fun or important to bring.

Was everyone included in making the decision? _____

How did you and your partner decide which of these items to bring on your camping trip?

_____
_____
_____

How could Tito, Lisa, and Richard use that strategy to solve their pizza problem?

_____
_____
_____

Let's think about seasons! Some activities only happen during certain seasons, like pumpkin carving in the fall or swimming outdoors in the summertime. Next to each season below are three different activities:

1. Circle the activity that you most want to do.

2. Now, you and your partner will need to pick one activity to do for each season. You will only have one minute to decide, so you will need to compromise quickly! Think about how you can use different kinds of compromising, like flipping coins, talking, or voting, to make your decisions.

Season	Activity 1	Activity 2	Activity 3	**Our** Choice
Spring	Pick flowers	Go to the zoo	Ride bikes	
Summer	Go to the pool	Go camping	Play basketball	
Fall	Pick apples	Watch football	Carve pumpkins	
Winter	Go skiing	Meet Santa	Make hot cocoa	

Was everyone included in making the decision? _____

How did you and your partner make your decisions?

_____

_____

_____

Let's See What We Learned!

Let's go back to the original comic. Look it over one more time and

come up with an idea for what you think should be in the comic.

What do you think should happen next?

Draw what you think the Kids should do:

Let's See What The Green Box Kids Came Up With!

Tito compromises by letting his friends have their own side of the pizza!

Lisa and Richard are looking forward to the pizza. Talk with your friends about their solutions.

Let's Learn About Compromise
Lesson 2: Afternoon Fun

Find out what you already know about compromise.

1. Does compromise always mean you get what you want? Explain.

_____

_____

_____

2. What are some things you can do if you and your friends are having a hard time finding a solution?

_____

_____

_____

3. Is compromise always "fair?" Explain.

_____

_____

_____

4. Why is compromise an important part of being a friend?

_____

_____

_____

5. You and a friend are at an amusement park. There is only time for one more ride before you leave. You want to ride the roller coaster. Your friend wants to ride a water ride. The two of you have to stay together. What could you do?

_____

_____

_____

Lesson 2: Afternoon Fun

Read the comic on the following page about Jack and Richard to learn about a time when friends were having a hard time finding a way to compromise. Make sure to look closely at the Green Box Kids' faces to see how they may be feeling.

Let's Break it Down!

Now we are going to break the comic down to get a better idea of what is going on in each picture.

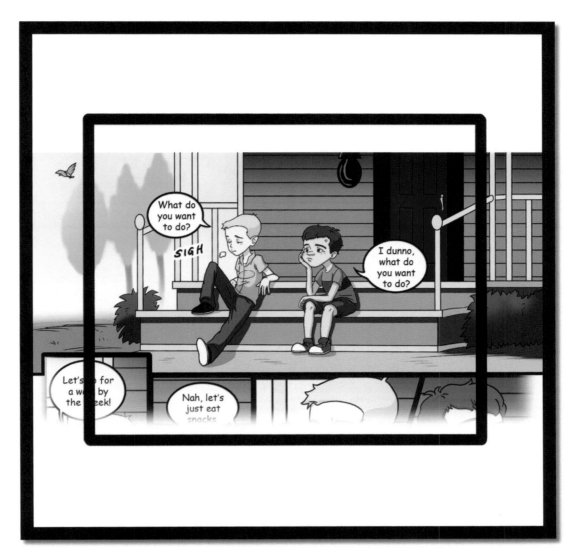

What is happening in this picture?

What is Jack's facial expression in this picture?

What is Richard thinking about?

What is happening in this picture?

How have their facial expressions changed?

Talk about their body language.

Let's Think About It.

The questions on the following page will help us better understand the

comic we just read.

Answer the following questions about the comic you just read. Some questions may have more than one right answer.

1. What did Jack want to do? What did Richard want to do?

_____

_____

_____

2. Why didn't Richard like Jack's suggestion?

_____

_____

_____

3. Why didn't Jack like Richard's suggestion?

_____

_____

_____

4. They couldn't find a compromise. Are either of the friends having fun?

_____

_____

_____

5. Are Jack and Richard angry with each other? How do you know?

_____

_____

_____

6. Should Richard just agree to take a walk by the creek?

_____

_____

_____

7. Should Jack just agree to eat a snack?

_____

_____

_____

8. Are there ways they could do both?

_____

_____

_____

9. Do you think Jack and Richard would have more fun together if they could figure out a compromise? Why do you think that?

_____

_____

_____

10. If they can't figure out a compromise, will this change their friendship?

_____

_____

_____

My way. Your way. Our way!

There are different possible solutions when we can't agree. Sometimes we can find ways that everyone can get what they want. In the next section we will talk about how we can find a good compromise.

Talk about it with your friends!

Can you think of a time when only one person could get what they want?

Why is it important to work together to find a compromise?

Use the Venn Diagram below to help you figure out solutions when:

- Only you can get what you want (**My way**).

- Only your friend can get what they want (**Your way**).

- There is a solution where both you and your friend get what you want (**Our way**).

For each problem, figure out a solution where only you get what you want (My way), only your friend gets what they want (Your way), and you both get what you want (Our way).

	My Way	Your Way	Our Way	Which is best?
There is only one slice of pizza left.				
You want to play Mario Kart®. Your friend wants to play Minecraft®.				
You and your brother both need the computer to finish your homework.				

Maybe Next Time. Sometimes we can't get what we want right now.

1. How does it make you feel when you have to wait until next time to get what you want?

_____

_____

_____

2. Is it fair if only one person can get what they want?

_____

_____

_____

3. What are some ways that we can still compromise?

_____

_____

_____

4. How could Jack and Richard still compromise if they can only either take a walk by the creek OR eat a snack?

_____

_____

_____

5. Is it okay to always be the one to get what you want?

_____

_____

_____

Here are some problems where only one person can get what they want <u>right now</u>. See what kinds of compromises you can find.

Problem	Compromise	Is it Fair?
Your family is getting take-out for dinner. You want pizza. Your mom wants Chinese food.		
Your family is planning a vacation. Your sister wants to go to the beach. You want to go to DisneyWorld®.		
You and your friend both want to be the pitcher in the last inning of the ball game.		
You are going to the movies. You want to see the new scary movie. Your friend wants to see the new cartoon movie.		

Let's See What We Learned!

Let's go back to the original comic. Look it over one more time and

come up with an idea for what you think should be in the comic.

What do you think should happen next?

Draw what you think the Kids should do:

Let's See What The Green Box Kids Came Up With!

Jack and Richard compromise by walking to the creek to have a snack picnic!

Jack and Richard are enjoying their afternoon. Talk with your friends about their solution.

Let's Learn About Compromise
Lesson 3: Band Practice

Find out what you already know about compromise.

1. How do you feel if a friend gets upset when you can't agree?

_____

_____

_____

2. What are some ways to tell friends your suggestions without getting angry?

_____

_____

_____

3. What does it mean to "fight fair" when trying to find a compromise?

_____

_____

_____

4. How does anger affect friendships?

_____

_____

_____

5. You and a friend are getting ready to play a game. Your favorite color is red. Your friend's favorite color is also red. Both of you want to use the red token. How do you feel if your friend ends up using the red token?

_____

_____

_____

Lesson 3: Band Practice

Read the comic on the following page about Tito, Barry, and Lucy to learn about a time when compromise did not go so well. Make sure to look closely at the Green Box Kids' faces to see how they may be feeling.

Let's Break It Down!

Now we are going to break the comic down to get a better idea of what

is going on in each picture.

What is happening in this picture?

Look at Barry's face. How is he feeling?

Talk about Tito's facial expression and body language.

What is Lucy's facial expression?

Is Tito checking in with his friends?

What is happening in this picture?

Let's Think About It.

The questions on the following page will help us better understand the

comic we just read.

Answer the following questions about the comic you just read. Some questions may have more than one right answer.

1. How did Lucy want to play the new song?

_____

_____

_____

2. Why did she want to play it that way?

_____

_____

_____

3. Why do you think Tito wanted to play it fast?

_____

_____

_____

4. Do you think Tito likes "jazzy" songs?

_____

_____

_____

5. How do Barry and Lucy feel about Tito's version of the song?

_____

_____

_____

6. How are Lucy and Barry feeling while Tito plays?

_____

_____

_____

7. What do you think Tito should do or say to make Barry and Lucy feel better?

_____

_____

_____

8. Should the band stay together or break up?

_____

_____

_____

9. Next time they have band practice, what could they do before they start practice?

_____

_____

_____

10. What can you do to make sure everyone has fun when you and your friends are together?

_____

_____

_____

Compromise Without Anger.

Compromising is about finding ways that everyone can participate in making decisions and finding solutions. In the next section we will talk about how compromise affects relationships.

Talk about it with your friends!

How do you feel when a friend doesn't listen to your suggestions when you are trying to find a solution?

How do you feel when others include you in their decision and try to make you happy?

Make it a "Fair Fight"

Sometimes it seems like our friends aren't listening to our suggestions and ideas. Sometimes it seems like they don't care about how we feel. When that happens, we might want to get mad.

If a friend yells or uses mean words, how does that make you feel?

_____

With a partner, think of some things you can say/do and some things that you should not say/do when trying to find a compromise.

Do	Don't
_____	_____
_____	_____
_____	_____
_____	_____
_____	_____

Let's make lunch! Mom wants us to make lunch. With a partner, decide on what to make for lunch. You can only pick one main dish, one fruit, one drink, and one dessert. Be sure to make it a "fair fight."

Our choices   ## We picked

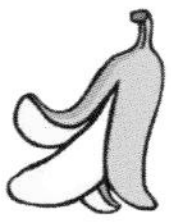

_____

_____

_____

_____

How did you and your partner decide what to have for lunch?

_____

_____

_____

How did you and your partner keep it a "fair fight?"

_____

_____

_____

How could Tito, Lucy, and Barry use your strategies to solve their problem?

_____

_____

_____

Let's See What We Learned!

Let's go back to the original comic. Look it over one more time and

come up with an idea for what you think should be in the comic.

What do you think should happen next?

Draw what you think the Kids should do:

Let's See What The Green Box Kids Came Up With!

Tito and Barry agree that Tito can have a one-minute loud and fast solo!

Everyone is enjoying band practice. Talk with your friends about their solution.

Appendix A:
Measuring Progress

Compromise Pre-Test

Before you begin using the lessons, use this pre-test to determine the child's current skill level.

The scales below describe different kinds of compromise scenarios. Rate HOW OFTEN the child engages in each behavior without any adult assistance. Base your ratings on recent observations.

Asks appropriately to compromise during a dispute (*Uses calm and apporiate language*):

Suggests an appropriate compromise solution (*Suggests a "middle ground," taking turns, etc*):

Remains calm during a compromise discussion (*Uses calm and appropriate language*):

Includes everyone in the decision-making process (*Listens to everyone involved, does not bully others into a solution, etc.*):

Accepts the outcome of a compromise discussion without problem behavior (*continues to participate in activity, does not complain about solution, etc.*):

Compromise Behavior Checklist

After you have completed the pretest, use this form to track development of compromise skills while using the lessons.

Instructions:

- Whenever you notice the child presented with an opportunity to compromise, use the form on the next page to:
  - Record the date.
  - Make notes about the activity. This could include the setting, who is present and/or how many other children are present, as well as what activities they are engaged in.
  - In the Skill section, make a checkmark in the box that most accurately describes the skill being displayed (note that these are also the skills assessed in the pretest).
  - In the Child's Response section, make a checkmark in the box that most accurately describe the way that the child responded.
    - Independently: Responded correctly without any adult assistance
    - Prompted: Responded correctly with adult assistance
    - Did not occur: A correct response did not occur
    - Problem Behavior: Some problem behavior occurred in response (does not remain calm, does not continue to participate, complains about situation, etc.)

Where to track skills:

- If you are using the lessons in a group format, use the form on the following page to track skills displayed in that setting.
- Other settings that you can track skills in:
  - Classroom
  - Home
  - Social groups (scout meetings, teams, clubs, etc.)

Measuring Progress:

- The goal is for the child to respond more frequently without adult assistance.
- If you are working with an ABA or other professional, you can share this information with them.

Extension:

You may continue to track the development of compromise skills after you have completed the lessons using this form.

Compromise Behavior Checklist

Date	Activity	Skill (check one)					Child's Response (check one)			
		Asks appropriately to compromise during a dispute	Suggests an appropriate compromise solution	Remains calm during a compromise discussion	Includes everyone in the decision-making process	Accepts the outcome of a compromise discussion without problem behavior	Independently	Prompted	Did not Occur	Problem Behavior

Compromise Post-Test

After finishing the lessons, use this post-test to determine the child's current skill level. DO NOT REVIEW THE PRE-TEST SCORES!

The scales below describe different kinds of compromise scenarios. Rate HOW OFTEN the child engages in each behavior without any adult assistance. Base your ratings on current behavior only.

Asks appropriately to compromise during a dispute (*Uses calm and approriate language*):

Suggests an appropriate compromise solution (*Suggests a "middle ground," taking turns, etc*):

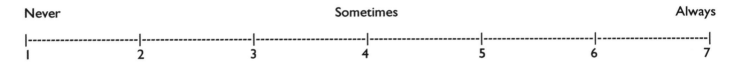

Remains calm during a compromise discussion (*Uses calm and appropriate language*):

Includes everyone in the decision-making process (*Listens to everyone involved, does not bully others into a solution, etc.*):

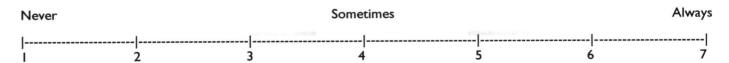

Accepts the outcome of a compromise discussion without problem behavior (*continues to participate in activity, does not complain about solution, etc.*):

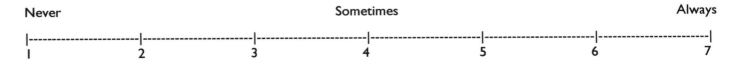

Pre-Post Comparison

- Fill in the chart below to compare compromise skills before and after using the lessons.

- To determine the degree of change (Change Score), subtract the pre-test score from the post-test score.

- For each item on the scale, more appropriate responses receive higher valued scores. Any change scores that are greater than 1, indicate that you have seen a change in that skill.

- Any skills that were scored lower on the Post-Test than the Pre-Test may need additional training. However, it is also possible that after using both the lessons and Compromise Checklist you are a more keen observer than before. This increased awareness to the types of responses the child is making may account for lower scores.
    - Compare the progress on the Compromise Checklist with the scores.
        - If the child is showing progress (more independent responses) on the Checklist, then progress is being made.
        - If the child is not showing progress on the Checklist, then additional learning opportunities and direct teaching is needed.

Skill	Pre-Test Score	Post-Test Score	Change (Post-test minus Pre-test) Score
Asks appropriately to compromise during a dispute			
Suggests an appropriate compromise solution			
Remains calm during a compromise discussion			
Includes everyone in the decision-making process			
Accepts the outcome of a compromise discussion without problem behavior			

Notes:

Appendix B:
Individualized Education Program Goals

Individualized Education Program Goals

The Individualized Education Program (IEP) is a document that defines the individualized objectives of a child who has been determined to have a disability that will impact their ability to receive an appropriate public education. Each IEP is tailored to meet the individual students' needs, as determined by evaluation (assessments and evaluations by school psychologists, standardized tests, performance on academic tasks, etc.). To meet those needs, the IEP includes measurable annual goals addressing each area of need.

As you have learned through these materials, compromise is a complex social skill that involves reaching an agreement during a dispute in which both sides making concessions, either through finding a "middle ground" or conceding something now in exchange for receiving something later. Children need to learn how to ask to compromise and how to respond when others ask.

Below are several suggested compromise goals. A good goal is one that is individualized for the student, reflects the student's current level of performance, and is a reasonable expectation for improvement over the course of the IEP year.

Sample Compromise Goal #1:
When given compromise scenarios, will identify the problem and suggest two solutions appropriate to the situation with no more than _____ adult prompts in _____ out of _____ opportunities for _____ consecutive days, as measured by teacher/staff data and observations.

Sample Compromise Goal #2:
During group activities, when presented with compromise/conflict situations, will state objections using appropriate language in _____ out of _____ opportunities for _____ consecutive days, as measured by teacher/staff data and observation.

Sample Compromise Goal #3:
During group activities, during compromise/conflict situations, will suggest an appropriate solution in _____ out of _____ opportunities for _____ consecutive days, as measured by teacher/staff data and observation.

Notes:

Appendix C:
For the ABA
Professional

Compromise

Use the materials in this book as a part of a comprehensive approach to teaching appropriate compromise skills.

Purpose: Increasing compromise strategies while decreasing maladaptive behaviors in contrived social scenarios.

Procedure:

The following are potential behaviors and goals. Successfully implemented Applied Behavior Analysis (ABA) therapy is individualized. Therefore, it is up to the instructor to determine the specific behaviors and goals for each student. Goals should be clear, concise, and easy to objectively track.

1. Define **behaviors** for each learner (use the data sheet on the following page). Examples (will vary on a learner by learner basis):
    a. "Identification of compromise situation" is defined as independently identifying whether it is appropriate or inappropriate to compromise in a given situation.
    b. "Appropriate compromise initiation" is defined as independently initiating a compromise negotiation using appropriate language.
    c. "Tantrum behavior" is defined as hitting, kicking, screaming, or eloping when asked to compromise.
2. Define **goals** for each learner for each behavior (use the data sheet on the following page). Examples:
    a. Compromise: Student A will suggest a minimum of 2 solutions to a compromise scenario as defined in the target.
    b. Tantrum: Student A will exhibit 0 tantrum episodes across 3 consecutive compromise scenarios for a given target.
3. Determine **targets** for each learner (use data sheet on the following page).
    a. Reduce the skill/behavior into smaller elements.
4. Use appropriate ABA procedures, such as prompts and prompt fading, errorless teaching, etc., to teach individual elements.
5. Use reinforcement to strengthen each new element.
6. Continue presenting opportunities until the learner(s) have mastered the goal at that target. We recommend continuing a target until the learner responds correctly on at least 80% of the opportunities for several consecutive sessions.
7. Use the suggested activities below to contrive opportunities to work on the targets.

Preferred Activity - Provide your students with a list of potential reinforcing activities (i.e., extra recess time, watching a movie, playing a game, etc.). Instruct the students to write down the option they would choose. When everyone has privately selected their preference, bring the group together and have the students share what they chose. Inform the students that they will have an opportunity to do only one of the activities, but only if the group can come to a compromise.

Neutral Activity - Assign a group project that requires the group to solve a difficult problem (i.e., dropping an egg from a height without breaking the egg). [A time limit may be added at the instructor's discretion]

Work Activity - Provide your students with a list of work activities. Instruct the students to write down the option they would choose. When everyone has privately selected their preference, bring the group together and have the students share what they chose. Inform the students that one work activity must be completed and that they need to compromise and work together to decide which one.

Student: _____

Behavioral Definitions and Goal(s):

Behavior	Definition	Goal

Target	Date Target Introduced	Date Target Mastered

About The Authors

Carl Dzyak, M.Ed. (Special Education, George Mason University), BCBA, LBA is the founder and CEO of Green Box ABA. He founded Green Box ABA, PLLC in October 2014. Carl has been a practicing behavior analyst since 2011 and has worked with individuals on the autism spectrum since 2007.

Barbara Kaminski, Ph.D (Psychology/Behavior Analysis, West Virginia University), BCBA-D, LBA is the ABA Clinical Director at Green Box ABA, PLLC. She teaches graduate level courses in ABA for both George Mason University and The Chicago School of Professional Psychology and maintains an Adjunct Faculty appointment at The Johns Hopkins University School of Medicine Department of Psychiatry and Behavioral Sciences. Dr. Kaminski has been working in clinical practice since 2013 and in the broader field of behavior analysis for over 20 years.

Chris Richardson, M.Ed. (Special Education, George Mason University), BCBA, LBA is COO of Green Box ABA, PLLC. He has been working in Applied Behavior Analysis since 2012 and has worked with children with special needs since 2007.

About The Artist

Sarah Miller began her art career with Game Design and Animation studies at The Art Institute of Washington, and later ended at George Mason University where she earned her Bachelor's of Individualized Study in Visual Arts and Narrative. She is a digital artist and game designer with a passion for creating, no matter its medium —there is nothing she loves more than bringing characters and worlds to life, "bridging connections between people with art and inspiration."

About Green Box ABA, PLLC

Green Box ABA, PLLC is an Applied Behavior Analysis (ABA) clinic located in Springfield, Virginia that provides innovative Applied Behavior Analysis therapy and high quality resources to clients seeking meaningful behavioral change. The therapy is rooted in science, but the approach is rooted in compassion.

63254599R00055

Made in the USA
Charleston, SC
01 November 2016